Alien Facts #10

BY ZEESHAN MAHMUD

TABLE OF CONTENTS.

	PAGE.
Anisandrus populi	22
Carphoborus carri	16
Crypturgus borealis	7
" *corrugatus*	7, 8
Eccoptogaster monticolæ	32
" *tsugæ*	32
Hylastes asper	19
" *nitidus*	19
" *scaber*	18
Hylurgops grandicollis	17
" *knausi*	17
" *lecontei*	16
Ips englemanni	30
" *hunteri*	31
" *yohoensis*	31
Leperisinus cinereus	15
Pholoeosinus canadensis	8, 9, 10
" *juniperi*	10
" *minutus*	9
" *rugosus*	10
Pityophthorus canadensis	24
" *confertus*	27
" *granulatus*	28
" *intextus*	29
" *lateralis*	27
" *nitidus*	25
" *nudus*	28, 30
" *ramiperda*	28
" *rhois*	26, 27
Pseudocryphalus, n. gen.	20
" *brittaini*	20
" *criddlei*	21
Pseudohylesinus, n. gen.	11
Pseudohylesinus sericeus	14
" *grandis*	11, 12, 13, 14
" *nobilis*	12
" *obesus*	15
" *sitchensis*	12
" *tsugæ*	11
Trypodendron borealis	21
" *rufitarsis*	22
" *ponderosæ*	22
Xyleborus affinis	24
" *canadensis*	24
" *inermis*	24
" *xylographus*	23

Extraordinary, THURSDAY and FRIDAY, Sept. 7, 8

Sessue Hayakawa in

The Vermillion Pencil

See the mighty volcanic eruption and earthquake merged into one of the most colossal spectacles of destruction ever screened!

See a whole city laid to waste by torrents of blazing lava.

Thousands of helpless natives fleeing to the uplands to escape the death-dealing flow. Huge buildings dashed to atoms by an earthquake when the aged Viceroy waves the——

All These And Other Terrific Scenes In One Of The Greatest Spectacles Of Disaster Ever Screened.

Brilliant cast, including Bessie Love and Ann May—Gorgeous Costumes—lavish sets and a love story of exquisite tenderness, in which the artistry of Hayakawa is beautifully exemplified.

ALSO OTHER GOOD SUBJECTS.

Pencil! While modern pencils are harmless, the word "pencil" actually derives from the Latin penicillus, meaning "little tail," originally referring to small brushes made from animal hair used for writing in ancient times. An unusual fact is that until the mid-19th century, graphite was mistaken for lead, a misconception that persists to this day even though modern pencils contain no actual lead.

This ancient art form is so culturally significant that it is listed as a Syrian intangible cultural heritage by UNESCO. In a fascinating display of versatility, some shadow play troupes perform by using the actors' own bodies as the shadows or by allowing the audience to view the performance from both sides of the screen simultaneously.

Manufacturers of Javanese wooden shadow puppets manufacturers at the pasar malam in Surabaya.

THE INVENTION OF THE FULL STOP (OR PERIOD) IS CREDITED TO THE GREEK GRAMMARIAN ARISTOPHANES OF BYZANTIUM AROUND 200 BCE.

制, 雕镂细致, 造型夸张, 具有浓厚的工艺
方特色。

Shadow Puppet

Shadow puppets are made of animal skin or cardboard, which are the exquisite folk arts and crafts as well. Shadow puppet is the shadow play on the screen in order to perform. Shadow puppet originated in Tang and Five Dynasties, flourished in Song, Yuan, Ming and Qing Dynasties and is developing until now.

Sichuan shadow puppet became popular in Daoguang and Xianfeng periods in Qing Dynasty. It was influenced by Beijing light shadow play and Shanxi light shadow play. The puppets are engraved with cowhide, the exquisite chasing and exaggerated shape of the shadow puppets represent the rich life spice and local features.

One of the most bizarre and poignant facts about shadow puppetry is its legendary origin: it was reportedly invented over 2,100 years ago as a way to summon the dead. According to Chinese legend, Emperor Wu of the Han Dynasty was so consumed by grief after the death of his favorite concubine, Lady Li, that he could no longer rule. A magician named Shao Weng claimed he could "bring her spirit back". He crafted a lifelike figure from leather, dressed it in her clothes, and placed it behind a silk screen lit by torches. When the Emperor saw the moving shadow, he was convinced it was his lost love, giving birth to the art of shadow play.

Other Bizarre Facts About Shadow Puppetry:
- The "Decade-Old" Leather: In Indonesia's premium Wayang Kulit (shadow theater), the most prized puppets are made from the

hide of a young female buffalo that has been cured for up to 10 years before it is even carved.
- Decapitation for Deception: In some versions of the Chinese origin legend, the Emperor eventually realized he had been tricked by the magician and had the man's head cut off.
- Marathon Performances: Traditional Indian Tholpavakoothu shadow plays (based on the Ramayana) can last for up to 41 consecutive nights to tell the full story.
- Ancient "TV": Because shadow puppets are projected onto a screen using light and movement, they are considered by many historians to be the direct ancestor of modern cinema and broadcast media.

Mathematically, falling raindrops oscillate in discrete spherical harmonic modes that act as a scattering "fingerprint," allowing polarimetric radars to distinguish between rainfall types by measuring the ratio of horizontal to vertical light scattering. These oscillations can even theoretically produce a rare "90° rainbow" in specific, uniform drop distributions, though this feature is usually smoothed away in nature by the random mix of different raindrop sizes.

Kurt Cobain: On Halloween night in 1993, Kurt Cobain performed a full concert in Ohio while dressed in a bulky Barney the Dinosaur costume. In an outrageous display, he chugged a bottle of Jack Daniel's through the dinosaur mask's mesh mouth during the show while his bandmates dressed as Slash, a mummy, and a "politically correct" version of actor Ted Danson.

Halloween: While modern Halloween is known for candy, it has roots in the 17th-century Massachusetts Bay Colony, where denying that the

Bible was God's word—a "spooky" thought to Puritans—was actually a crime punishable by death as of 1646. During this same century, belief in the supernatural was so intense that the Salem witch trials led to over 200 accusations and 19 executions for "spectral" crimes. *Facemask:* Beyond their medical use, masks have a bizarre history in performance and politics; for instance, Zambian "witchdoctors" were arrested as recently as late 2024 for possessing charms and "knowledge of witchcraft" while allegedly attempting to bewitch the country's president. In historical 17th- century Europe, masks and hoods were also a standard part of the executioner's attire, such as when the killer of King Henry IV was publicly pulled apart by four horses.

This figure is of the nduda type, characterized by the attached "guns" loaded with gunpowder and used to shoot witches. It is the only figure that adopts the threatening pose: the right hand raised, holding a spear or knife, and the left hand resting on the hip. Two guns protrude horizontally on both sides of the cylindrical medicine pack on the belly, covered with a round piece of mirror.

Bizarre 17th-Century Incident

In one of the most unbelievable historical events of the 17th century, the corpse of Oliver Cromwell — who had died of natural causes in 1658—was exhumed in 1661 by order of King Charles II for a "posthumous execution". His decaying body was ritually "hanged, drawn, and quartered" at Tyburn, and his severed head was stuck on a pole outside Westminster Hall, where it remained for over 20 years as a warning to rebels.

Weird TikTok Bizarre Video Fact

A strange and viral TikTok trend in 2025 involves creators using specialized drone photography to capture "impossible" angles of abandoned or bizarre locations, such as a marooned pleasure boat in a dried-up lake bed. These videos often focus on "dead" landscapes or contaminated sites like Kabwe, Zambia—labeled the most lead-polluted place on Earth—where the haunting visuals of toxic dust have garnered millions of views as part of a "disaster tourism" digital subculture.

de Goden in verken-schotten gebragt, met deze woorden daer over t'uiten: *Dit geven wy u, onze Goden, om onze zwijnen te bewaren en vet te maken.* Voor haer moeite krijgt de duyvel-jaegster tien bos pagie, een vadem geschildert kleet: de rechter schouder van ieder verken, een stuk des zwijns buik, een stuk van 't hert, lever, nieren, een weinig reusels en *Masakhaw*: eindelijk word zy verzocht van alle daegs tot hunne huizen te komen, om te bidden, dat zy lang mogen staen. Een zulke kracht schryven de Formosanen deze offerhande toe, dat sy geloven dat geen duyvel of geest hen nochte hunne huizingen kan beschadigen of quaet doen.

Zoo by ongeval brand in deze huizen komt t'ontstaen, (waer door dikwils heele buurten ja dorpen, door de lichte onvonkbaerheit der stoffe, aen kolen raken) de schult wort op den eersten man geleit, dien zy op straet vinden, schoon zulx niet waer is. Dees moet daer voor vergoeding van schade tot heropbouwing geven: is hy onwillig, zijn huis wort hem verbrant: wort'er niemant gevonden, ieder biet den gene, wiens huis verbrant is, de behulpelijke hant in het heropbouwen.

In dezer wijze worden de huizen op de vlakte gebout, maer die op de bergen zijn gelijk zwijnekotten.

Wat belangt de magt en sterkte dezes eilants: het is zeer manrijk: want haest onmogelijk is te brengen de grote meenigte des volks in rekening. De Steden, door het geduurig oorlogen tegen elkandre, zijn met allerlei vonden van vastigheden gesterkt: en omringt, in plaets van muuren, met dikke en vaste bosschaedjen, veel vaster en sterker, dan eenige wallen of muuren: want de bomen in de bosschaedjen, zijn zeer dicht en tot over de drie hondert treden in de brete geplant.

D'uit en ingang is slechts een kruispadt, met vele bochten en omwegen, daer niet meer als man voor man door

Sterkte des Eilands.

Soap Opera

While most people view soap as a modern hygiene staple, 2.6 million bars of soap are discarded daily by the hotel industry in the U.S. alone. In a bizarre historical twist, 17th-century European physicians often advised **against using** soap for bathing, fearing that it opened the pores to "corrupt air" and diseases like the plague, leading many elites—including King Louis XIV—to reportedly wash only their hands and faces while avoiding a full-body lather for years.

Candle: In an unbelievable display of biological utility, the "candlefish" (Eulachon) is so naturally oily that indigenous peoples of the Pacific Northwest used to dry the entire fish, thread a wick through it, and burn it as a real, literal candle.

Historically, candles were also used as "alarm clocks"; owners would drive metal nails into the wax at specific intervals so that when the candle burned down, the nails would clatter loudly onto a metal tray below to wake them up.

Nebuchadnezzar:

King Nebuchadnezzar II, the most powerful ruler of ancient Babylon, is famously recorded in the Bible as having suffered from a bizarre seven-year bout of boanthropy—a psychological disorder where he believed he was an ox.

During this time, he reportedly abandoned his throne to live in the wild, grew hair like eagle feathers, developed claws like a bird, and exclusively ate grass until his "sanity" was restored.

Oat:

For centuries, oats were considered a lowly weed and "diseased" wheat by the ancient Romans, who used them exclusively as horse feed and scoffed at Germanic tribes for eating them. This perception was so enduring that Samuel Johnson's 1755 dictionary famously defined oats as a grain "eaten by people in Scotland, but fit only for horses in England," and it wasn't until a 19th-century marketing blitz that Americans were convinced to eat what they previously considered "livestock fodder."

Flume: In the 19th century, loggers built massive "V-shaped" water flumes that stretched for miles across mountain ranges, but the most outrageous use of these was "flume sliding," where workers would ride small wooden boats or even just planks down the chutes at terrifying speeds of up to 60 mph. These makeshift "water slides" were incredibly dangerous; in 1876, two journalists famously survived a 15-mile white-knuckle descent down a California flume in just 30 minutes, an event that helped inspire the modern log flume amusement park ride.

Bizarre Incident in Togo

In a truly unique and unbelievable cultural phenomenon, Togo is home to the Akodessewa Fetish Market, the largest voodoo market in the world, where you can buy "magical" items ranging from monkey heads to elephant feet. A bizarre incident involving the country's national identity occurred in 1974 when

President Gnassingbé Eyadéma survived a high-profile plane crash that killed everyone else on board; claiming he survived through supernatural protection, he immediately used the incident to launch a "Togolization" campaign, ordering all citizens to drop their Western names in favor of African ones within 24 hours.

Bizarre Fact: Number 22 and November 1921

On November 22, 1921, a fascinating and eerie coincidence occurred involving the number 22: the legendary explorer Sir Ernest Shackleton was in the midst of his final Antarctic expedition, having set sail on a ship that was exactly 22 tons in weight. This specific date in 1921 marked a pivotal moment in his journey where he recorded the crew eating a breakfast of Quaker Oats—a brand whose founder, William Penn, famously became a Quaker at the age of 22—just weeks before Shackleton suffered a fatal heart attack on the ship.

Weird Instagram Story Fact

A strange and viral Instagram trend in 2025 involves "Deliciously Ugly" stories where users post intentionally unappetizing photos of their food to protest the platform's history of "perfect" aesthetics. This movement gained massive traction after a fashion influencer wore a dress made entirely of dried oatmeal to London Fashion Week, leading to a bizarre surge in "oatmeal-core" stories where millions of users shared videos of themselves "hatching" candy dinosaur eggs from their breakfast bowls to trigger 90s nostalgia.

Toucan: *Although a toucan's massive, neon-hued beak can account for up to half of its body length, it is not a heavy weapon but a high-tech "thermal radiator" that acts like a living air conditioner. These birds can adjust the blood flow to their beaks to radiate as*

much as 100% of their body heat—a cooling efficiency four times greater than that of an elephant's ears—and they must tuck their beaks under their feathers at night to prevent freezing while they sleep.

Paperweight: In a bizarre historical "lost and found" cycle, the complex technical knowledge required to make **millefiori** ("thousand flowers") glass paperweights was completely lost to humanity by the 18th century, despite having been mastered by the ancient Egyptians as early as 1400 BCE. The secret to creating these intricate patterns was only rediscovered in the 19th century, sparking a Victorian obsession that saw collectors like Oscar Wilde and Empress Eugénie treating these glass baubles as the ultimate high-status desk accessory.

Founder of Hologram: Dennis Gabor, the "Father of Holography," actually gave up on his invention and considered it a failure in 1955, years before the laser even existed to make it functional. He won the 1971 Nobel Prize in Physics for a concept he originally developed by accident while trying to improve electron microscopes, ultimately proving his own famous mantra: "You can't predict the future, but you can invent it".

Dhow: These ancient sailing vessels are traditionally constructed using a method that defies modern engineering: the planks are often sewn together with coconut fiber rope rather than being held by nails. This "sewn boat" technique allows the hull to remain flexible, enabling the dhow to survive grounding on sandbars or crashing through coral reefs without the rigid wood snapping under pressure.

Fight Circus: Based in Thailand, **Fight Circus** is a combat sports promotion that treats professional fighting like a surrealist fever dream, featuring sanctioned bouts such as "two-on-one" matches, blindfolded boxing, and "musical chairs" grappling. Perhaps its most bizarre offering is the "Wheel of Misfortune," where fighters must endure absurd handicaps, such as fighting while handcuffed or while holding a leg of ham, turning elite martial arts into a literal carnival of chaos.

In 12th-century England, the village of Woolpit was the site of a truly unbelievable event: the appearance of the **Green Children of Woolpit**, two siblings who reportedly had bright green skin and spoke an unrecognizable language. According to medieval chroniclers, they refused all food until they discovered raw broad beans, and once they learned English, they claimed to have come from a subterranean world called "St. Martin's Land," where the sun never shone and everything was green.

A fascinating coincidence involving the number 33 occurred in January 1923, when the world-renowned physicist Albert Einstein arrived in Palestine for his only visit to the region. At exactly 33 years old, just a decade prior, Einstein had published the foundation of his General Theory of Relativity, and during this 1923 trip, he was officially presented with the news of his Nobel Prize—which he had actually won for the year 1921—while staying at a house located at No. 33 on a prominent local street.

In the realm of modern digital absurdity, one of the weirdest hashtag facts involves the trend #Planking, which reached a bizarre peak when it evolved into "Extreme Planking" in dangerous locations. This cultural phenomenon became so surreal that a man was actually arrested in 2011 for "planking" on a police car, while another fan of the trend made headlines for successfully planking on the moving blades of a wind turbine, proving that the internet can turn a simple physical act into a life-threatening, one-of-a-kind spectacle.

Sew me!!!

Sewing is one of the world's oldest textile arts, fundamentally altering human evolution by allowing early ancestors to survive harsh climates and eventually express social identity.

Prehistoric Origins (50,000–10,000 BCE)

The earliest known sewing tools were not crafted by modern humans alone.

The First Needles: The world's oldest known sewing needle, made from bird bone and dating back roughly **50,000 years**, was discovered in Siberia's Denisova Cave. It is attributed to the **Denisovans**, an extinct human species.

The "Eyed" Revolution: The invention of the "eyed" needle—featuring a hole to carry thread—emerged approximately **45,000 years ago** in Siberia and China.

Materials: Before metal, needles were fashioned from bone, antler, ivory, and even thorns. "Thread" consisted of animal sinew, catgut, veins, or plant fibers like raffia.

Survival and Fashion: Sewing allowed humans to stitch animal hides into fitted garments, essential for migrating into colder northern regions. Evidence suggests these early stitches were also used for decorative embroidery and ornaments as early as 30,000 years ago.

Evolution of Tools and Materials

As civilizations progressed, sewing technology became more sophisticated:

Ancient Egyptians significantly advanced the craft by spinning flax into linen to sew garments and sails for international trade.

- **Metal Needles:** Iron needles appeared around the **3rd century BCE** in Germany. By the 14th century, steel needles were being manufactured in Europe, though they remained a luxury for centuries.

- **The Thimble:** The oldest known thimble dates to the **Han Dynasty (202 BC–220 AD)** in China, used to push crude needles through tough leather.
- **Textiles:** The sewing of woven cloth began around **4000 BCE** in the Middle East.

The Industrial Shift (18th Century–2025)

For millennia, sewing remained a laborious manual task predominantly performed by women in domestic settings.

The First Machine: Thomas Saint patented the first sewing machine design in **1790**, though it was intended for leather and canvas.

The Lockstitch: In **1846**, Elias Howe patented a machine using the lockstitch mechanism, which became the industry standard. Isaac Singer later refined this in the 1850s, making machines affordable for households.

Modern Era: In 2025, sewing has transitioned from a survival necessity to a widespread creative hobby. Modern technology now integrates **AI pattern**

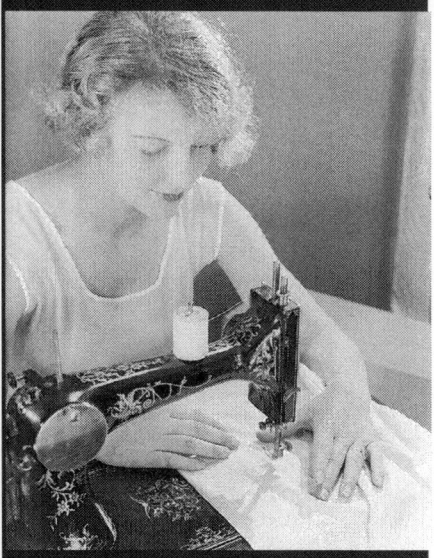

generators, 3D garment previews, and digital communities that allow hobbyists to build global brands from home.

POST YOUR PHOTO WITH THE HASHTAG

#FOUNDALIENFACTS AND YOU MAY EARN A CHANCE TO BE *FEATURED* ON OUR NEXT EDITION!*

*Restrictions apply. Must be 18 and over!

Longest ingredient list in the world?

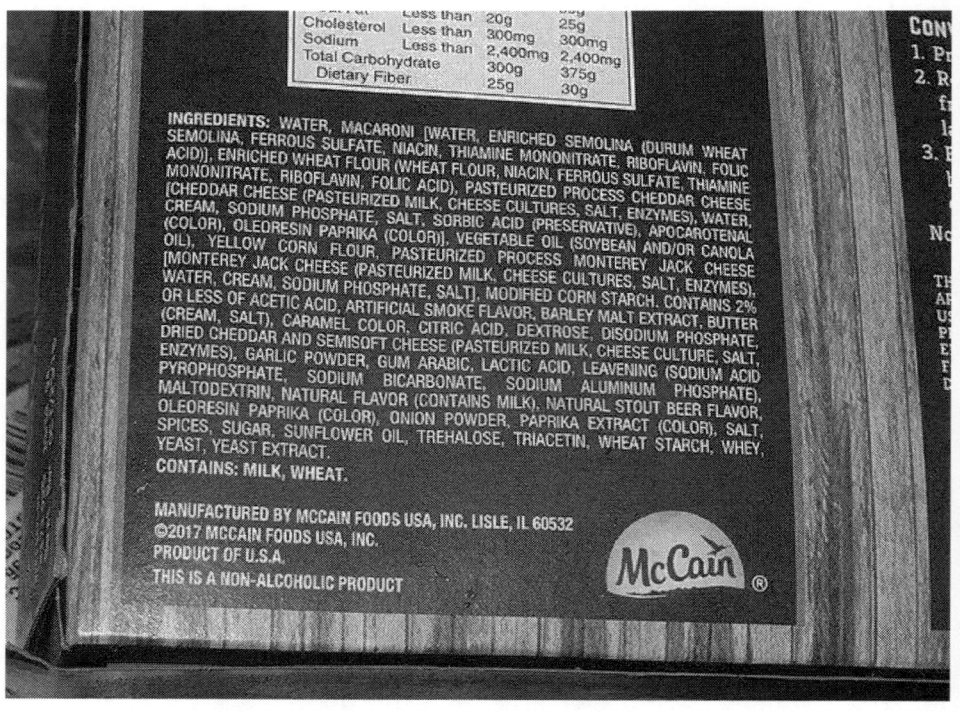

Made in the USA
Coppell, TX
20 January 2026

68745838R00016